# THE LI
# KIRKPATRICK

CW01513245

# A Dumfriesshire blacksmith
# who invented a bicycle

Cover photo of Kirkpatrick, with children Mary and
John, in 1860. Reproduced by permission of the
Local Studies and Archives Service, Dumfries and
Galloway Council.

## by David Hurdle

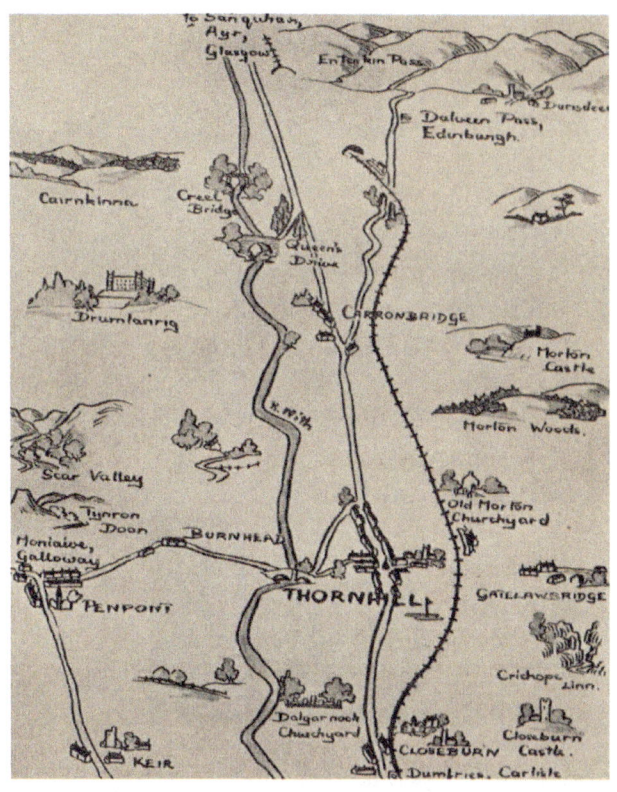

Thornhill Village Committee (no longer in existence), 'A Guide to Thornhill', undated

**Map of the Thornhill area showing Keir, Thornhill, the River Nith and the Lowther Hills**

# CONTENTS

# CHAPTER 1  INTRODUCTION

*"One of the most important days of my life, was when I learned to ride a bicycle."*

**Michael Palin, actor**

Reproduced by permission of the Local Studies and Archives Service, Dumfries and Galloway Council.

**Kirkpatrick's home, Courthill Smithy**

W hy am I writing this? Well, I was born in Dumfries and have strong family connections with the area. I learnt to ride a bicycle there during a childhood summer holiday in 1953. And more recently I discovered that my late uncle's great grandfather's brother-in-law was, you've guessed it, Kirkpatrick Macmillan. So, I wanted to find out what life was like in the 1800s in Dumfriesshire and specifically to learn more about Kirkpatrick's life (1812-1878) as a local blacksmith.

I begin by setting the scene, what rural life was like and what he actually did; Kirkpatrick certainly was not just a blacksmith, vital as that was to the community. I then explore his family and why so many children died so young. Kirkpatrick lost two plus his wife in just four months.

I finish with a short summary of the effect his bicycle has had and the extensive network of cycle routes now available in Dumfriesshire. I hope that visitors to Scotland, including to the places where there are now replicas of Kirkpatrick's bicycle, can now take away a straightforward account of his life and his achievement.

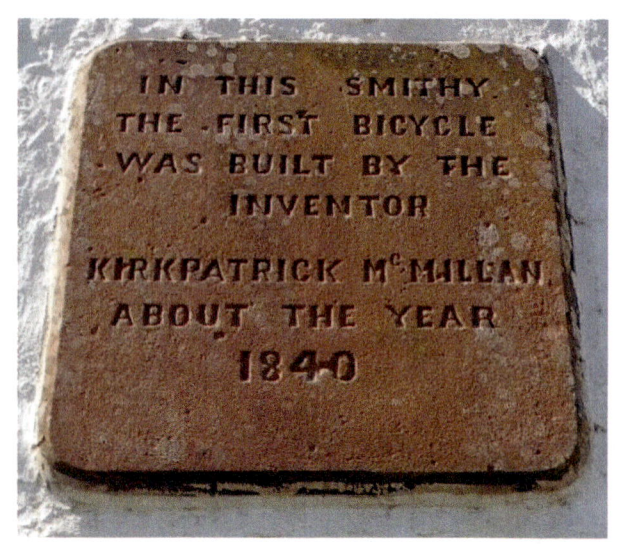

David Hurdle

David Hurdle

**The plaques on the wall of Courthill Smithy**

I must point out that many aspects of the story of the invention of the bicycle are subject to controversy, but what follows is a fairly popular interpretation of events based on -

Research published in 1899 by a James Johnston.

Interview by writer/journalist/broadcaster Gordon Irving of Kirkpatrick's son John in about 1940.

A book by Andrew Ritchie in 2009 called The Origins of the Bicycle Kirkpatrick Macmillan, Gavin Dalzell, Alexandre Lefebvre published by the John Pinkerton Memorial Publishing Fund. It contains a wealth of information, source material and evidence.

# CHAPTER 2   VICTORIAN LIFE IN NITHSDALE

*"When the spirits are low, when the day appears dark, when work becomes monotonous, when hope hardly seems worth having, just mount a bicycle and go out for a spin down the road, without thought on anything but the ride you are taking."*

**Arthur Conan Doyle, author**

## Revolutions

This chapter describes what life would have been like for Kirkpatrick growing up and working in Dumfriesshire in the 1800s.

The century was characterised by an agricultural and then an industrial revolution. The Agricultural Revolution was a gradual transformation of the traditional agricultural system that began in Great Britain in the 1700s. Aspects of this complex transformation, which was not completed until the 1800s, included the reallocation of land ownership to make farms more compact and an increased investment in technical improvements, such as new machinery, better drainage, scientific methods of breeding and experimentation with new crops and systems of crop rotation. However, the agricultural boom did not last, with the onset of a depression from the late 1870s.

The Industrial Revolution, roughly 1760 to 1830, was the transition to new manufacturing processes in Europe and the United States. Great Britain was the first industrialised nation in the world. The Revolution's second half saw major developments in transport, first canals; and then railways initially mainly for freight, not passengers.

Textiles were the dominant industry of the Industrial Revolution in terms of employment, value of output and capital invested. The textile industry was also the first to use modern production methods. In Scotland in 1815 most workers were employed in textiles.

## Life in Dumfriesshire

Imagine life in the rolling countryside of Dumfriesshire in the 1800s. Few decent roads, no cars, vans or lorries as they had not been invented; horses pulling mailcoaches from town to town, a largely farming community with cattle, horses and sheep. But the rural world *was* beginning to develop, with more mechanisation; and railways were starting to be built. This was the kind of life that Kirkpatrick was born into.

Kirkpatrick's small village was Keir Mill in the parish of Keir. It is 2km (1.2 miles) south east of Penpont, 3.2km (2 miles) south west of the village of Thornhill which is at the heart of the district, 22.5km (14 miles) north of Dumfries and 19km (12 miles) south of Sanquhar. In 1684 there were only 18 people living in Thornhill, but this number grew when the Dumfries–Glasgow Road was built near it, in 1715. Thornhill's population nowaday is about 1,500.

David Hurdle

**The River Nith between Thornhill and Keir Mill**

David Hurdle

**Nithsdale's hills**

*The Buccleuch and Queensberry Hotel*
*Thornhill, Dumfriesshire    1856*

Hotel table mat

**A sketch of the hotel and cross in 1856, looking south**

Thornhill Village Committee's 'A Guide to Thornhill', undated, photo credited to A Shuttleworth

**Thornhill's lime tree lined main street in early Spring, looking north in the 1950s**

The mercat cross[1] in the centre of Thornhill was erected by the Duke of Queensberry in 1714 and is a fine example of its kind. It is

---

[1] A **mercat cross** is the Scottish name for the market cross found frequently in Scottish cities, towns and villages where historically the right to hold a regular market or fair was granted by the monarch, a bishop or a baron. It therefore served a secular purpose as a symbol of authority and was an indication of a burgh's relative prosperity. Today there are about 126 examples existing in Scotland.

octagonal and surmounted by a fluted Corinthian column, formed of local sandstone and topped by a lead figure of the winged horse Pegasus. The lead was mined in nearby Lead Hills.

David Hurdle

**The centre of Thornhill showing the Buccleuch and Queensberry Hotel and the mercat cross**

Annual fairs were held in the district from 1610 till 1747. In 1715 the Duke of Buccleuch built an inn but the present Buccleuch and Queensberry Hotel was built in 1851. I actually lived there for a few months in 1946 as my grandparents and my mother ran it after the war. Thornhill's land is owned by the Duke, whose home, Drumlanrig Castle, is 4.8km (3 miles) away.

The castle was built between 1679 and 1690 by the first Duke of Queensberry on the site of an older castle. After the death of the 4th Duke of Queensberry ownership passed to the 3rd Duke of Buccleuch. In 1873 a 'List of Owners of Land in Scotland' showed that the 5th Duke of Buccleuch was the largest owner of land in Dumfriesshire by far. Nowadays his estates amount to 1,100 sq km (280,000 acres), nearly 40% of the county's land area; and he is the largest private landowner in Scotland.

David Hurdle

**Drumlanrig Castle**

There were few roads in Scotland until the late 1700s. Travellers used simple, well-known routes, drove roads, paths and tracks. Most things were moved on people's backs or by packhorses; and cattle moved themselves. Auctions catered for the sale of animals and from the 1880s cattle marts became common in small towns.

The railways from about the 1840s onwards improved communications. They helped to transform Great Britain from a rural to an urban society, from an agricultural economy to an industrial one. This all contributed to the steady erosion of the need for fairs, once essential for people to gather together to buy and sell goods, stock and agricultural produce.

Thornhill used to be served by train, sited on the London to Glasgow line via Carlisle, Dumfries and Kilmarnock. Dumfries station opened on 23rd August 1848 and the line to Glasgow in 1850. Thornhill station opened on 28th October 1850. Certain London trains stopped at Thornhill on request. The station closed on 6th December 1965 but re-opening it has been considered in recent years.

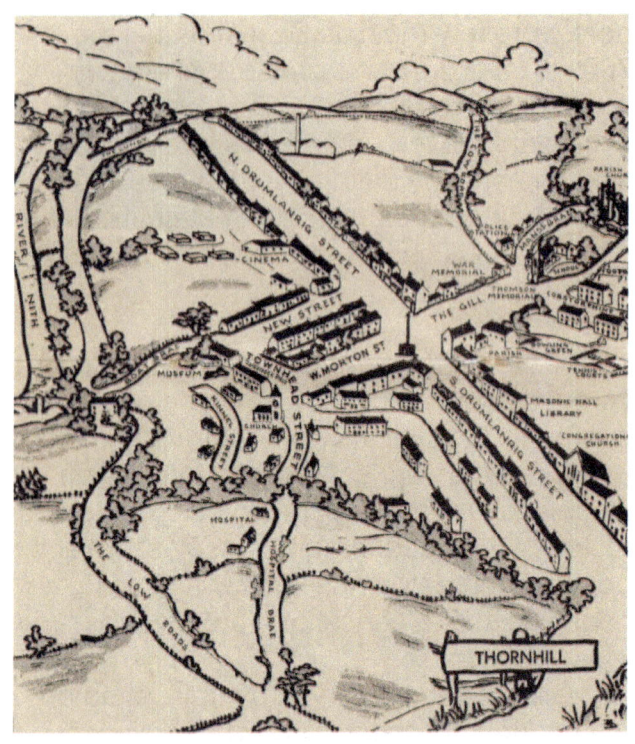

Thornhill Village Committee's 'A Guide to Thornhill', undated

**A diagrammatic map of Thornhill showing the main, wide street, mercat cross and River Nith**

A hundred years ago, a 1922 guide book to west and south west Scotland recognised the attractiveness of the area to cyclists. Thornhill is described as *".... A place of some charm as being in the centre of a most attractive district both for the cyclist and the pedestrian. The village itself is said to be one of the neatest and best kept in Scotland"*. A cycle route from Thornhill to New Galloway and Newton Stewart is described as *".... A splendid route, and one that should certainly not be missed in fine weather by any cyclist desirous of getting an idea of the wild country ...."*.

During Kirkpatrick's lifetime, 1812 – 1878, the development of a rail network and the widening of the market for products, clearly helped farming in Dumfriesshire to prosper. Villages during the 1800s would comprise joiners, shopkeepers, wheelwrights, blacksmiths, and shoemakers. Many women were lace-makers, dressmakers, milliners, spinners and weavers. Itinerant hawkers and pedlars travelled from village to village selling small household and agricultural wares; or doing seasonal work. Certain industries flourished during the 1800s; in fact, hand-knitting was common throughout Scotland from the early 1600s. Once power-operated knitting machines became available the domestic craft became an industry.

In chapter 4, I mention the deaths in Kirkpatrick's family. There was no National Health Service of course until 1948. Whereas smallpox had been a major killer in the 1700s, in the 1800s it was tuberculosis/consumption. During *each* decade of Queen Victoria's reign, it claimed between 60,000 and 70,000 lives in Great Britain. The 1800s also saw various other outbreaks, such as cholera in Dumfries in 1832 when nearly 500 people died, and in 1848 (when 65 out of 180 died), and in Langholm in 1849. And there was a severe drought and consequent water shortage in 1852.

Despite the above setbacks, by the 1860s Great Britain's economy was booming. Agriculture had done well for about twenty years but depression set in from the 1870s. In the mid-1800s nearly one in three of the male population of Scotland worked in farming. More people worked in agriculture than in mining and textiles combined. But at the end of the century farming accounted for just one in seven of the population. Rural population reached a peak in 1850-1870 but by 1950 had fallen to the levels of the mid-1700s. However, total population *was* rising. The first government census in Scotland in 1841 recorded 2.6 million, about double the number estimated in 1775. In 2019 it was 5.5 million.

# The town of Dumfries

Kirkpatrick's nearest town was Dumfries, 13km (8 miles) from the mouth of the River Nith at the Solway Firth. It was created a royal burgh in 1186 and is nicknamed Queen of the South. It was a flourishing market town by the 1400s. There were the usual craftsmen – fleshers, skinners, glovers, shoemakers and bakers. However, being close to the border with England it did suffer in the 1300s and 1400s during conflicts with England and got burned several times, including in 1448 and 1536.

From the 1600s, possibly earlier, the town was the main collecting point for cattle from Nithsdale and held weekly markets and three annual autumn fairs. It remained a busy market town and port until about 1800. Then in the 1900s the port went into decline. However, the population grew rapidly, from 10,069 in 1841 to 13,710 in 1871, and by 1951 to 26,323; today it is 31,600.

David Hurdle

## Dumfries, the River Nith and a cycle path alongside

Dumfries's attraction is well summed up in a pamphlet by the Scottish Motor Traction Company many years ago – *"Dumfries has associations with King Robert the Bruce, Burns, Carlyle and Scott. Situated on the banks of the Nith, immortalized by Burns, in a country highly picturesque, few Scottish towns can lay claim to a more historic past or a more inviting present".*

# 1812 – 1878 (Kirkpatrick's lifetime)

1825 – On 27th September, the world's first steam locomotive passenger service ran between the towns of Stockton and Darlington. It ushered in the 'Railway Age', with the building of an extensive railway network in Great Britain providing a faster and economical means of transport and communication.

1833 – Records show that shipping trade at Dumfries was as follows: imports – coal, slate, iron, timber, tallow, hemp and wine; exports – wool, freestone, oats, wheat, barley.

1835 – Founding of Dumfries's museum and astronomical observatory, including the camera obscura, the oldest of its type still in use in the world today.

1837 – The Dumfries and Maxwelltown Total Abstinence Society was formed. By 1838 membership had reached 1,500.

1839 – Dumfries experienced a hurricane.

1845 – A Dumfries Soup Kitchen opened to minister *"…. to the wants of all and sundry, but particularly the industrious serving, suddenly thrown out of employment…."*.

1848 – Dumfries's first stretch of railway between there and Gretna Junction opened on 22nd August. The first train left at 11.30am with two locomotives and thirteen carriages.

1859 – The Dumfries to Castle Douglas railway opened.

1871 – The North of England and the South of Scotland felt an earthquake.

# CHAPTER 3   THE ROLE OF A BLACKSMITH

*"He builded better than he knew."*

**Plaque put on wall of Courthill Smithy in 1939**

David Hurdle

**Courthill Smithy, Kirkpatrick's home**

## A pillar of the community

In rural life a blacksmith was a very important person. No community could exist without one. Their work involved heating iron and steel in a forge and then beating it into shape with hammers. The forge burnt charcoal or coal at high temperatures. The sort of work they did would include making and repairing a wide range of agricultural implements and tools such as blades for ploughs, fittings for carts, iron tyres and hub caps for cart wheels, hoops for barrels, hand tools, cooking pots, other domestic utensils, gates and chains. They also mended a cracked frying pan, fashioned a decorative wrought iron gate or made a new tooth for a gear wheel.

Each forge would have a water trough for cooling things, and bellows to blow air over the fire to make it burn at higher temperatures. The bellows would be operated with one hand while iron was held in the fire with tongs using the other hand. An anvil would be used to hammer iron into shape.

To early people the working of metal seemed magical, so blacksmiths held a lot of power and there were superstitions, maybe why horse shoes are thought to bring good luck? Blacksmiths were certainly held in high regard in their community, seen as leaders, solving local disputes and even carrying out marriages. There were often no veterinary surgeons for many miles so if any farmers had ailing animals, whether cattle, horses, dogs, cats, they were immediately sent for.

Kirkpatrick used to show his wares at a big Highland Show in Dumfries. He would make and sell things for the farming community that were different, such as ploughs without screws. He even made some agricultural implements for *"Mr Gladstone, of Capenoch, near Penpont, a brother of the ex-Premier"*. His son John recalls how his father *"made several improvements to the plough"* and exhibited at the *"Dumfries Highland Show"*.

In 1862 a newspaper listed a small item in its list of implements exhibited – *"Mr Kirkpatrick M'Millan, Courthill, Keir – malleable iron swingle-trees, made by exhibitor"*. Swingle-trees are a part of the mechanism connecting a plough, or other arm equipment, to the horses.

David Hurdle

**Courthill Smithy, Keir Mill, nowadays a private residence**

## Horses galore

Let's be clear. Before there were tractors, cars, vans and lorries all farm machinery and vehicles were pulled by horses. They were the primary source of power for agriculture, mining, transport (pulling mailcoaches, trams and buses) and warfare, until the arrival of the steam engine. Even by 1900 there were 3.3 million in the UK of which one million were working horses, a third of which in agriculture. By the Second World War the number had halved (as had the number of blacksmiths). In 2017 there were 258,459 horses in the UK of which 34,599 were in Scotland.

In the 1800s agriculture and transport needed thousands of them. And they all needed iron shoes made by blacksmiths. They were fitted to the hoof, then replaced every three months. In some areas cattle were also shod before they started on the long journey to market. So a blacksmith was crucial in a rural community.

# CHAPTER 4   THE MACMILLAN FAMILY

*"When I see an adult on a bicycle I have hope for the human race."*

**H G Wells, author**

## Kirkpatrick's parents

Kirkpatrick was born on 2nd September 1812 in the small village of Keir Mill in the parish of Keir. The entry in the Old Parish Register for Keir gives a baptism date of 18th. He was the son of Robert Macmillan, from Morton and Mary (née Auld) from Keir. Robert was born on 3rd September 1778 and Mary in 1782 or 1783; her father was a saddler. They married in Keir on 18th October 1800. Robert was a blacksmith like his father. Robert died on 4th February 1854, aged 75, Mary on 18th July 1860, from 'natural decay', aged 77. Kirkpatrick was 6th of 10 (or possibly twelve) children.

The name of Kirkpatrick was given to him by his parents out of respect for, and in the memory of the family name of Sir Thomas Kirkpatrick, 5th Baronet of Closeburn, Sheriff of Dumfriesshire from 1811 to 1844, who had shown a kindly interest in the Macmillan family.

# Kirkpatrick's siblings

Research using www.familysearch.org reveals that Robert and Mary had ten children over the 21 years from 1802 to 1823. John was the first in 1802, then Robert in 1804, but he died in 1817, just 13. 1806 saw James; 1808 Walter, who died in 1837 from consumption, aged 29. 1810 saw George Hoggan, then 1812 Kirkpatrick, 1814 Jean, 1819 Mary, 1820 Isabella, and 1822 Anne. Some information is unclear on some of these but certainly:

- It was a very big household.
- Some did not reach adulthood.

The main survivors, apart from Kirkpatrick, were brothers John, George Hoggan, and James, and sister Isabella.

The above reflects the experience of many families in the 1800s in Great Britain:

- No contraception so often ten or more children.
- One after the other was the norm.
- Children dying young.

Until the 1800s, 40% of children did not reach adulthood. Furthermore, a child had a 12% chance of *both* parents being dead by the time he/she was 25. In 1800 life expectancy at birth was only in the high 30s, but by 1900 had reached 48. Today it is 79 for men and 83 for women.

The Macmillan family were reckoned to be clever and intelligent. Two of Kirkpatrick's elder brothers, John and George Hoggan, became teachers; John was classics master at the High School of Glasgow after having spent seven years teaching Greek and Latin at Dumfries Academy; and at one time was tutor to an MP, John Bright. At the time of his death, he was rector of Edinburgh High School. George Hoggan was second master of Hutcheson's Grammar School. In the 1841 census George Hoggan is recorded as living in the Gorbals area of Glasgow in a cabinet maker's household of seven. Another of Kirkpatrick's brothers, James, was a clerk in a Glasgow warehouse. The 1841 census shows him as residing in Rutherglen, a town near Glasgow.

Isabella was born in 1820, married George Marchbank[2] (born 1816) from Morton on 8th

---

[2] The Marchbanks are my link to Kirkpatrick as my uncle was a Marchbank.

March 1839, and died in 1864, aged 45. They lived in Closeburn, a village between Dumfries and Thornhill. George was a precentor at the parish church at Closeburn. A precentor facilitated worship such as leading the congregation in singing or prayers. He died on 2nd January 1856, aged 39, in Closeburn after a drunken brawl. Isabella and George had six children, all girls, over sixteen years, Mary in 1839 who must have died very young as a second Mary was born in 1840; Jane in 1849; Agnes in 1850; Annie in 1853; and Sarah in 1855.

## Kirkpatrick's early years

Although Kirkpatrick attended school, he did not acquire most of his education until he was 30 and attended a night school (see chapter 6). His first work was as a farm labourer where he learnt to plough, and also grew to love horses. Farm boys tending horses could start work as early as 5am, feeding and preparing them for their day's work. Other farm workers would usually start work at 7am and work till 6pm. A horse boy's lunchtime break could be longer than for the other workers, as he would be seeing to the horses, who needed to rest and be fed, and his day might not end till 8pm. Whilst Sunday would be a farm worker's day off, the horse boy still had to feed the horses, so did a seven-day week.

At 17, Kirkpatrick got the opportunity of becoming a groom and coachman to a rich, local man, breaking in and training horses. This was at Holywood, close to Ellisland Farm, the home of Robert Burns twenty years before Kirkpatrick was born. He excelled at the breaking in of young horses, trying them out on the road to Moniaive where ponies and the occasional mailcoach were the only traffic. *"In appearance Kirkpatrick was tall - fully six foot – and of a muscular and wiry build"*.

However, smithy work was his lifetime's ambition, the calling of his father and grandfather before him. So his parents were delighted when another fine opportunity came his way – to become an apprentice to the chief blacksmith at nearby Drumlanrig Castle, the seat of the Duke of Buccleuch, 6.1km (3.8 miles) away. He learnt to forge iron and fashion wood and made friends with another apprentice John Findlater, who worked at the Wallyford Smithy near Thornhill and also on the Buccleuch Estate. In the evenings, they got together in Kirkpatrick's dad's smithy. They decided as a project to construct a hobbyhorse, a walking machine that had been invented by the German Baron von Drais. It was favoured by ladies and gentlemen of the aristocracy.

## Marriage and children

The Macmillan family were devout, and strict, Presbyterians. Kirkpatrick was very critical of people who smoked and drank alcohol. He used to give smithy apprentices a couple of shillings or half-a-crown if they would stop smoking. His son John has told how he refused to let the family even read on a Sunday.

The 1851 census shows Kirkpatrick living with his parents, Robert and Mary, sister Anne, a nephew, James and a niece Mary Marchbank. There were also two teenage apprentices, one of whom was a nephew, William. The Valuation Rolls of 1855 list Kirkpatrick as a 'tenant occupier' of 'the farm of Courthill'.

Kirkpatrick married Elspeth, or Elsie, Gordon Goldie on 24th April 1854 at Keir. She was a lady's maid to the Hunter-Arundell family at the nearby Barjarg Tower, a castle and mansion built in about 1680. How did they meet? Well, the story goes that he was called over to do some work on their horses and afterwards was invited into the kitchen for a mug of tea. Six servant girls were preparing the evening meal for the Arundell family.

Given his style of making jokes, Kirkpatrick strode jauntily into the kitchen, smiled at the lassies, and blurted out in a semi-jocular manner – *"Say, lassies, is there ony yin here that'll mak' a guid wife tae me?"* One of the girls, Elspeth, knew this was her chance and in a quiet voice said simply – *"I will"*. They got engaged a few weeks later. There is evidence that Kirkpatrick formally proposed marriage when they were enjoying a trip to Edinburgh together. An entry in the parish records shows dates for proclaiming Banns but not the actual date of the wedding.

Elspeth was born in 1833 so was 21 when she married Kirkpatrick; he was 41. She died of tuberculosis on 28th July 1865 aged just 32, having born six children over nine years:

| | | |
|---|---|---|
| Mary Lilias | born 1855 | died 1856 |
| Annie Christina | born 1856 | died 1857 |
| Mary Lilias | born 1858 | died 1928 |
| Robert | born 1859 | died 1865 (1) |
| John | born 1862 | died 1955 |
| Kirkpatrick | born 1864 | died 1865 (2) |

---

(1)  6 years old on 1st November from tuberculosis, just three months after his mother died.
(2)  One year old on 3rd October 1865 from 'Whooping cough, months and bronchitis, weeks', just ten weeks after his mother died.

The 1861 census shows the household as Kirkpatrick, Elspeth, daughter Mary, son Robert, Kirkpatrick's sister Ann, aged 40, a domestic servant, and a blacksmith's apprentice, David, aged 19. The 1871 census shows still, Kirkpatrick, daughter Mary and son John, and Kirkpatrick's sister Ann; a different apprentice, Joseph Thompson, aged 16; and a nephew Robert.

Sadly, only two of Kirkpatrick's and Elspeth's six children reached adulthood, daughter Mary, who became a teacher and son John, a policeman. Of their six children three died within 14 months of their birth. After Elspeth's, Kirkpatrick junior's and Robert's deaths in 1865, three deaths in four months, Kirkpatrick, understandably, lived a quiet life turning his attention to designing, making and improving farm machinery.

By the 1871 census, he was a widower, living with just two children, Mary and John, sister Anne, two apprentices, one of whom was a nephew named Robert.

He was a great character, and in addition to several inventions was well known in the district as a 'grand whistler', unqualified dentist (pulling the teeth of humans *and* horses and cattle), designer of ploughs[3], fiddle player at weddings, and harmonium player. He was sociable, good humoured, teetotal, a devout, seriously minded Christian, with a puritanical streak and a strong work ethic.

Kirkpatrick attended church all his adult life and joined the Free Church of Scotland after the schism with the Church of Scotland in 1843. The schism, or disruption as it became known, was based on the importance of church democracy to congregations, and the right for churches and dioceses to appoint their own Minister. The newly established Free Church split from the established Church to have this right, and Kirkpatrick became a member of the Free Church.

Writer/journalist/broadcaster Gordon Irving wrote a biography of Kirkpatrick in 1986 and had met Kirkpatrick's son John in about 1940. John was the only remaining link with Kirkpatrick. Gordon in his book includes quotes from John about his father. One about his teeth-pulling skills is pertinent to repeat here. John recalls:

---

[3]A plough he designed used a pin device to make it easier to work and manoeuvre and was exhibited at the Dumfries Agricultural Show, most probably in the 1860s.

*"On the kitchen shelf at Courthill there stood a big bottle something like those seen inside the windows of sweet shops. When my father died, this bottle was within an inch off the top of being filled with teeth that he had pulled, for he acted as a local dentist as well as blacksmith in his day. The teeth in the bottle didn't represent one quarter of those he had drawn, for people used to take those he had pulled away with them. He used to lance the gum first before pulling the tooth, and gas, of course, was unknown in those days."*

At some point, John moved to Lancashire and the 1891 census records him as a 29 year old police constable in Liverpool and lodging, with five others, with his sister Mary at Toxteth Park. Twenty years later, aged 49, the 1911 census has him living in Smithdown Road, Toxteth Park. He was now a Labour Master at the Toxteth Park Workhouse. The workhouse was at the 'New Female Imbecile Hospital'. When he retired, he eventually lived in a care home, the Belmont Road Public Assistance Institution. He died on 18th November 1955.

David Hurdle

**Signpost to Keir Mill cemetery**

Like many people in the 1800s, Kirkpatrick died of consumption; on 26th January 1878 at 9.30 in the morning. His son John, 15 at the time, was present at his bedside. Kirkpatrick has been added to the family tombstone, after Elspeth, Kirkpatrick junior and Robert.

David Hurdle

**General view of cemetery showing the (white) Macmillan tombstone**

KIRKPATRICK MACMILLAN 1813 - 1878

Blacksmith in Keir for most of that time.

In the nineteenth century, a blacksmith was a pillar of his community. He fashioned the complete range of ironwear that the community used – from ploughshares to cartwheels to horseshoes to door latches and other domestic requirements. Many performed other important functions, even pulling teeth.)

Macmillan certainly lived up to that prominence and usefulness. He is credited with making improvements to agricultural machinery and, of course, he turned his hand to inventing the world's first pedal bicycle.

His gravestone gives us an insight into social history of the time. In the tragic year of 1865, he lost his wife aged 32, a baby, and his 6 year old son. He himself lived to 65, and his parents into their 70s, but the gravestone illustrates how often communities experienced the deaths of children and young people.

This plaque and the two fingerposts into the cemetery were subscribed to by The Centenary Club and unveiled on May 12, 2006.

David Hurdle

**The plaque, Keir Mill cemetery**

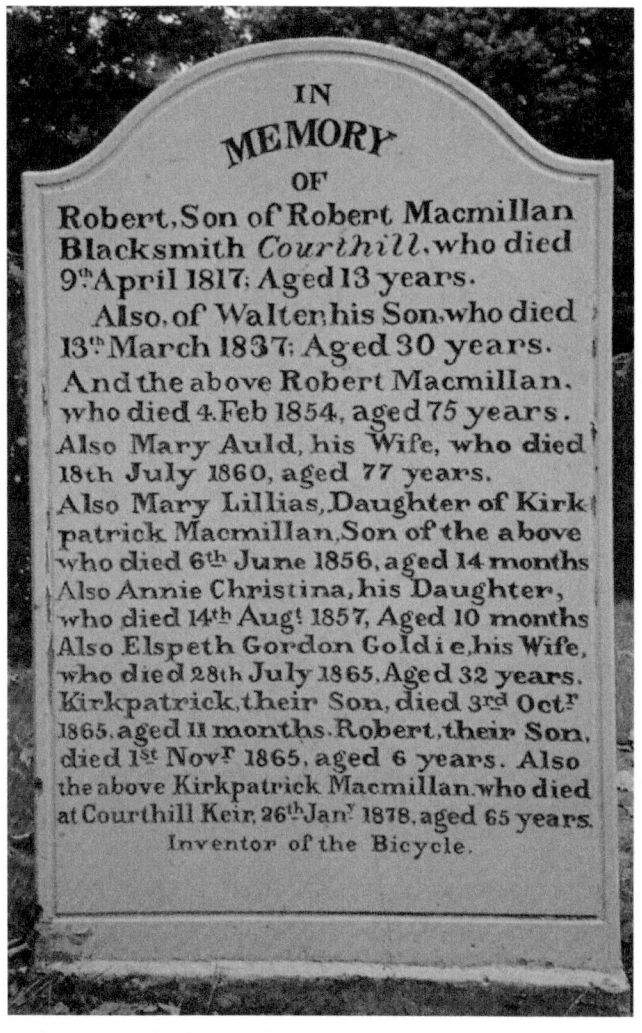

IN

**MEMORY**

OF

Robert, Son of Robert Macmillan
Blacksmith *Courthill*, who died
9th April 1817; Aged 13 years.
  Also, of Walter, his Son, who died
13th March 1837; Aged 30 years.
And the above Robert Macmillan.
who died 4 Feb 1854, aged 75 years.
Also Mary Auld, his Wife, who died
18th July 1860, aged 77 years.
Also Mary Lillias, Daughter of Kirk
patrick Macmillan, Son of the above
who died 6th June 1856, aged 14 months
Also Annie Christina, his Daughter,
who died 14th Augt 1857, Aged 10 months
Also Elspeth Gordon Goldie, his Wife,
who died 28th July 1865, Aged 32 years.
Kirkpatrick, their Son, died 3rd Octr
1865, aged 11 months. Robert, their Son,
died 1st Novr 1865, aged 6 years. Also
the above Kirkpatrick Macmillan, who died
at Courthill Keir, 26th Jany 1878, aged 65 years.
Inventor of the Bicycle.

David Hurdle

**Family tombstone, Keir Mill**

41

# CHAPTER 5   THE INVENTION

*"You always know when you're going to arrive. If you go by car, you don't. Apart from anything else, I prefer cycling. It puts you in a good mood, I find."*

**Alan Bennett, Playwright**

## From hobbyhorse….

Kirkpatrick Macmillan is regarded as the first person to fit pedals to a bicycle. He invented such a machine in 1839-40. Sometime in the late 1820s, he went to repair a farmer's plough near Carronbridge, a village north of Thornhill, saw a hobbyhorse being ridden along a road and decided to make one for himself.

In some history books the story goes that Kirkpatrick was prompted when a hobbyhorse was brought into his smithy to be repaired. Anyway, having built a machine he realised that there was scope for significant improvement.

The hobbyhorse had existed in Germany and Great Britain and enjoyed a brief craze in about 1817 to 1820. It had to be moved along by pushing your feet on the ground. Kirkpatrick thought what a radical improvement it would be if he could propel it without putting his feet on the ground.

Courtesy Science Museum

**Example of a hobbyhorse**

Eventually, he completed his new machine, with his friend, John Findlater, in about 1839, aged 27. The first bicycle with pedals, it was propelled by a horizontal reciprocating movement of the rider's feet on the pedals. This movement was transmitted to cranks on the rear wheel by connecting rods.

Before long, Kirkpatrick was regularly to be seen riding the 22.5km (14 miles) between his home and Dumfries. Fellow villagers thought Kirkpatrick 'mad' for dreaming up such an idea and he became known locally as Daft Pate, a crazy inventor. Pate was a contraction of Kirkpatrick spoken in strong Dumfriesshire lilt.

## ....to velocipede

David Hurdle

**A model of Kirkpatrick's velocipede at the Joseph Thomson Local Heritage Centre, Penpont**

This model in the Joseph Thomson Local Heritage Centre, Penpont, was made by local resident Eric Keggans in 2014. Joseph was an African explorer and the heritage centre, which was his home, contains a lot of information about him but also about the locality's culture, and personalities such as Kirkpatrick.

Kirkpatrick's invention in 1839-40 was basically a pedal driven bicycle made of wood, with iron-rimmed wooden wheels, a steerable wheel (760mm, 30 inches) in the front and a rear wheel (1,016 mm, 40 inches) connected to pedals via connecting rods. It weighed 26kg (57 lbs). It was quite different from hobbyhorses with wooden wheels shod with iron tyres and the frame consisted of a curved wooden backbone, forked to accommodate the rear-driving wheel and carry the axle bearings near its end.

The steering-wheel was carried in an iron fork, whose pivot passed through the frame and had the handlebar attached to it. The rear axle had cranks keyed to its ends and these were driven by connecting-rods from intermediate points in two swinging levers, pivoted near the steering head and carrying wooden treadles at their lower ends.

### Replica of Kirkpatrick's velocipede

Kirkpatrick's machine was known as a velocipede, a human-powered land vehicle with one or more wheels. The most common type nowadays is the bicycle. The term was probably coined by Charles, Baron von Drais de Sauerbrun, in French as vélocipède for the French translation of his advertising leaflet for his version of the 'laufmaschine' (German for running machine). That was also known as a 'dandy horse' which he had developed in 1817 and first rode on 12th June that year. His invention got called a Draisienne in France.

A 14.5km (9 mile) trip took Charles under an hour, less time than a mail coach. He obtained a local patent by January 1818 and was granted a five-year French patent by February. It was the world's first balance bicycle and was soon popular in the United Kingdom, first seen by the Spring of 1819, and in France. It was made entirely of wood and metal.

David Hurdle

**The information panel on the wall of Courthill Smithy**

London's Science Museum has summed up progress in the mid-1800s –

*"The twenty years which followed the invention of Macmillan's bicycle have little or no records by means of which the development of the cycle during this period can be accurately assessed. Certain isolated examples of original designs exist, however, which suggest that experimentation with the cycle was by no means abandoned and that, possibly, quite material advances were achieved …. It is almost impossible to determine which of these specimens actually anticipated their particular historical prototype, and which were merely crude later copies. They are, nevertheless, of significance in showing that a definite undercurrent of interest and endeavour existed before the first commercial cycles appeared in France after 1860 …."*

# CHAPTER 6   THE RIDE TO GLASGOW

*"I thought of that while riding my bicycle."*

**Albert Einstein, on his Theory of Relativity**

## Gearing up

Kirkpatrick, and John Findlater, tried the invention out on their local roads, attracting much interest. Kirkpatrick soon mastered the art of riding it and managed the 22.5km (14 mile) trip to Dumfries in under an hour. Sometimes he had his niece Mary Marchbank on his shoulders (the world's first female pedal cyclist?). His next exploit was to ride the 109km (68 miles) to Glasgow in June 1842 to visit his two schoolteacher brothers, one of whom lived in The Gorbals. He set off on the evening of 6th June. The trip took him two days, spending a night at Old Cumnock with John Mckinnell, the parish schoolmaster and friend of his brothers from their student days.

## The incident

Arriving in Glasgow he had ridden on rough, pot-holed roads on a machine weighing 26kg

(57 lbs). Robert Dinwiddie wrote, in his Guide to Dumfries in 1935 that:

*"We are told that his progress by the way caused great wonder and excitement. He was escorted into the city by an immense multitude of people, attracted by the strange novelty of the steed and its rider. To escape from the crowd Macmillan rode his machine on to the footpath, and unfortunately, he knocked down a child, for which offence he was fined 5 shillings at the Gorbals Police Court on 8 June 1842".*

This incident has been reported by others, who refer to a slight injury to a small girl who ran across his path in The Gorbals area. He was arrested, granted bail and went to stay with his eldest brother until his appearance the next day at the Barony Court. The charge was – *"Riding along the pavement on a velocipede to the obstruction of the passage and the danger of the lieges; and in so doing, having overthrown a child".* The Glasgow Argus on 9th June 1842 reported *"a gentleman from Dumfries-shire bestride a velocipede of ingenious design".* The magistrate was dumbfounded at his speeding – 13kmh (8mph) – lecturing him that *"This modern craving for speed is something to be deplored, I must say. A man riding a machine of two wheels and making it progress without having to touch the ground, I just can't believe it. The highways of this country will soon not be safe to travel on".* He was fined five shillings, equivalent to a couple of days wages. The 'gentleman' is not named but many believe that it was indeed Kirkpatrick.

The magistrate was impressed with Macmillan's bicycle and asked him to perform a figure-of-eight demonstration in the courtyard outside. The full text of the newspaper's report is:

> *"Yesterday, a gentleman, belonging to Dumfries-shire was placed at the Gorbals police bar, charged with riding along the pavement on a velocipede, to the obstruction of the passage, and with having, by so doing, thrown over a child. It appeared, from his statement, that he had on the day previous come all the way from Old Cumnock, a distance of 40 miles, bestriding the velocipede, and that he had performed the journey in the space of five hours. On reaching the Barony of Gorbals, he had gone upon the pavement, and was soon surrounded by a large crowd, attracted by the novelty of the machine. The child who was thrown down had not sustained any injury; and, under the*

*circumstances, the offender was fined only 5 shillings. The velocipede employed in this instance was very ingeniously constructed – it moved on wheels turned with the hand, by means of a crank; but, to make it progress, it appeared to require more labour than will be compensated for by the increase of speed. This invention will not supersede the railways."*

## The aftermath

It is said that the judge personally slipped him the money to pay the fine. It has to be said that there are some doubts about the accuracy of some of the above in this chapter; it depends whose book on the history of bicycles that you read. For one thing the press report of the court case did not name the offender; also, in those days it was unlikely that a blacksmith would be considered a gentleman. And word had it that when Kirkpatrick left the city, at the boundary he met a stagecoach going to Carlisle. They agreed to race each other on the 20 or so miles to Kilmarnock. Apparently, the stagecoach was soon left behind. But bear in mind that the stagecoach had to stop from time to time to set down and pick up passengers. As on the way *to* Glasgow he stayed the night at Old Cumnock.

Kirkpatrick's original machine passed into the possession of a nephew living in Thornhill who, not realising its historic importance, broke it up and destroyed it. Kirkpatrick did make some more in the next few years for friends, though none survive.

Legend has it that Kirkpatrick became known as The Devil on Wheels, partly on account of the rumbling of the velocipede's iron wheels on the rough, otherwise quiet, country roads. *"Aye, it's the verra De'il himself"* was the cry of mothers plucking their offspring to bosoms and hurriedly yelling *"ben the hoose"*. And the street vendors in Glasgow apparently called attention to the city's newspapers by shouting *"Devil on Wheels! Devil on Wheels! The Devil comes to Glasgow riding on a Hobby-Horse!"*

Back to the facts, and the 1841 census shows Kirkpatrick living in Glasgow with his elder brother John. He worked at the Vulcan Foundry, part of Robert Napier's shipbuilding and engineering empire. Napier was well known for encouraging his apprentices to attend night school before going on to become engineers. At about 30 Kirkpatrick would not have been too old to be an apprentice in the foundry by day and studying at night. His son John has said that *"It was his boast that he received most of his education by attending a night school when he was thirty years of age"*.

Eventually, he decided the city was not for him and returned home to help his father who was aged 66 by now. In 1854 two things happened. Kirkpatrick's father died on 4th February, aged 75; and Kirkpatrick, now aged 41, married Elspeth Goldie, aged 21, two months later in the April.

# CHAPTER 7   THE EFFECTS

*"As a kid I had a dream — I wanted to own my own bicycle. When I got the bike, I must have been the happiest boy in Liverpool, maybe the world. I lived for that bike. Most kids left their bike in the backyard at night. Not me. I insisted on taking mine indoors and the first night I even kept it in my bed."*

**John Lennon, musician**

## Other bicycles

As Kirkpatrick did not patent his invention it was inevitably produced by other people. There are real doubts as to who invented the first bicycle. It is unlikely ever to be solved. What does seem fairly clear is that Kirkpatrick invented the first bicycle with pedals; previously, on a dandy horse, and hobbyhorse, the rider had to propel it by pushing along the ground with their feet.

The popularity of cycling in the second half of the 1800s led to a publication written in about 1869 by an engineer, Andrew Muir, on 'The Velocipede: How to learn and how to use it'. The pamphlet said that speeds of 10 to 15 miles an hour could easily be obtained. As today the health benefits were recognised. An Indian velocipede called The Rantoone could do 8 to 12 mph. Muir notes that a professor wrote that *"On a good road, I can go twenty miles without the slightest fatigue. The Rantoone is not only valuable as a means of locomotion, but as a gymnasium it is perfect, giving equal work to all the muscles of the body. For this reason, it is especially useful in India, where exercise is the exception, when it ought to be the rule".*

The first mass produced pedal-equipped bicycle was made by the Michaux company from 1857 to 1871. It was sometimes called the boneshaker as it was made entirely of wood, then later with metal tyres. During the 1870s advances in metallurgy led to the development of the first all-metal velocipedes. Penny-farthings became very common in the UK in the 1880s. The term velocipede became a collective term for various types of bicycle development between 1817 and 1880. It refers especially to the forerunner of the modern bicycle that was propelled, like a modern tricycle, by cranks, i.e. pedals, attached to the front axle, before the invention of geared chains and belt and shaft drives powering the rear.

1878 saw the establishment of the Bicycle Touring Club, later changing its name to the Cyclists' Touring Club and in 2016 to Cycling UK. Today there are over 70,000 members, see www.cyclinguk.org

## Replicas of Kirkpatrick's

Replicas of Kirkpatrick's machine are in the Dumfries Museum and Camera Obscura; Loreburne Shopping Centre, Dumfries; Drumlanrig Castle; Riverside Museum, Glasgow; and the Science Museum, London. The replica bicycle at Dumfries's Museum was exhibited at the National Exhibition at Crystal Palace in 1896.

## Research

Although Kirkpatrick never patented his machine or capitalised on his invention the secretary of the Glasgow Cycling Club in 1892 credited him with the invention of the bicycle or the 'geared dandy horse' as it was known by some

Gavin Delzell (or Dalzell) was a wheelwright from Lesmahagow, Lanarkshire. It is said that he copied Kirkpatrick's machine in 1846-47 and passed on the details to so many people that for more than 50 years he was generally regarded as the inventor of the bicycle. Gavin's design incorporated the same general features as Kirkpatrick's but had a different frame and backbone. In the 1890s James Johnston, a corn trader and tricyclist, and member of the Glasgow Tri-cycling Club, undertook extensive research and received a gracious letter from Gavin Delzell's son acknowledging Kirkpatrick as the true inventor. The letter, dated 16th April 1892, read:

> *"Dear Mr Johnstone, As the result of the enquiries you have made into the question of the earliest inventor of the bicycle or geared dandy-horse, I have no hesitation in frankly admitting that you have proved that Kirkpatrick Macmillan constructed his one before my father constructed his, Yours very truly, J B Dalzell".*

Johnston has also identified Kirkpatrick as the gentleman fined in Glasgow in 1842. However, scepticism does remain.

The Dumfries and Galloway Standard on October 10, 1896, noted:

> *"...Mr James Johnston, of Glasgow, a well-known Dumfriesian, has just presented to the Observatory the duplicate of the first bicycle made by Kirkpatrick Macmillan,*

*blacksmith, Keir, which has for some time been on view at the Crystal Palace. It will be placed in the Observatory in about a fortnight, and should prove an interesting addition to the already numerous attractions of the place."*

In 1899, James Johnston wrote an article, 'The First Bicycle', in the Winter edition of a local magazine The Gallovidian. In it he stated his aim of:

*"…. to prove that to my native county of Dumfries belongs the honour of being the birthplace of the invention of the bicycle".*

Johnston did not present conclusive proofs, though he wrote that he had them. In his 1899 article he recalls how a -

*"….great number of old residents still residing in Dumfriesshire remember the man and his wonderful 'horse' well, so called from a prettily carved head he had affixed in front of his machine. A native of that county, writing from Toronto, Canada, in 1892, said he knew Macmillan well, and remembered him performing a journey to Glasgow in the early forties' on a visit to three of his brothers resident there…."*

Johnston also recalls meeting an elderly gentleman in 1897 in Dumfries who saw Kirkpatrick and his bicycle going through Kilmarnock on his way to Glasgow.

# CHAPTER 8   CYCLING TODAY

*"The bicycle is the most civilised conveyance known to man. Other forms of transport grow daily more nightmarish. Only the bicycle remains pure in heart."*

**Iris Murdoch, author**

## The benefits of cycling

There can be no doubt that cycling is good for your health and the environment. Nowadays, as we address various emergencies – air pollution (at illegal levels in many places), climate change and COVID-19 (2020 – 2022) cycling has been making a comeback as its benefits are realised and increasingly accepted.

Today, we now have some good government strategies and policies in place supportive of cycling. From a 'Cycling and Walking Investment Strategy'; 'Gear Change, A bold vision for cycling and walking'; 'Gear Change: One year on'; 'Cycling Infrastructure Design' guidance and good practice for local authorities; to a 'Decarbonising Transport' White Paper. Cycling is now seen as an essential part of a 'green recovery' for addressing air pollution and carbon reduction, as well as supporting heathier travel. Prime Minister Boris Johnson summed up the way forward in July 2020, four months into the COVID-19 pandemic:

> *"I have always known that millions more people in this country want to cycle, if the conditions are right, and the past four months have proved it. The joy of cycling is that doing it doesn't just benefit you. It doesn't just make you happier. It doesn't just make you healthier. It helps millions of others too, whether or not they have any intention of getting on a bike. It means less pollution and less noise for everyone. It means more trade for street-front businesses. It means fewer cars in front of yours at the lights".*

More and more local authorities are now implementing cycle paths and routes, and secure parking facilities. More schools and employers are encouraging cycling. But there are huge variations both within the UK and among countries. Why do 55% of Cambridge residents cycle at least once a week, and 26% in Exeter, but only 4% in Croydon?[4] In the rest

---

[4] https://www.gov.uk/government/statistics/walking-and-cycling-statistics-england-2019

of Europe 27% of all trips in The Netherlands are by bike, 22% in Hungary, 16% Denmark and Sweden, 13% Finland and 12% Germany. The UK? Less than 2%.[5]

In 1977, Sustrans was formed. Cycling was now being taken much more seriously. Sustrans is an engineering charity and the custodian of a National Cycle Network, a UK-wide network of traffic-free paths for cyclists, also walkers, connecting cities, towns and countryside. The Network comprises 20,540km (12,763 miles) of signed cycle routes throughout the UK. Scotland has 2,644km (1,643 miles). Sustrans works with schools to encourage 'active travel' (cycling, walking or scooting) among students. It also works with employers and local authorities. It administers about 4,000 volunteers who contribute their time to the charity in numerous ways, such as cleaning and maintaining the National Cycle Network, enhancing biodiversity along the routes, leading walks and rides and supporting communities to improve their air quality.

In Scotland, Sustrans has established partnership teams, embedding officers in local councils as well as NHS Scotland, the Scottish

---

[5] https://ecf.com/cycling-data

Environment Protection Agency, Scottish Natural Heritage and Transport for Edinburgh.

2.6 million bicycles were sold in the UK in 2019; and sales of e-bikes are increasing – from 40,000 in 2015 to 101,000 in 2019.[6]

David Hurdle

**A cycle route in Nithsdale, the KM trail to Drumlanrig Castle**

---

[6] https://www.cyclinguk.org/statistics

# Cycling in Dumfriesshire

Certainly, Dumfriesshire is a delightful place to cycle. The country lanes are very quiet and the hills not too steep. If they are you can always push your bike, which many cyclists do not seem to realise! I often watch them struggle when they do not need to.

David Hurdle

**Drumlanrig Castle's beautiful setting**

To celebrate the 150th anniversary of Kirkpatrick's invention, the KM Cycle Trail was implemented in 1990. It is a 22.5km (14 mile) signed cycle route between Dumfries and Drumlanrig Castle. There are now several cycle trails at the castle.

David Hurdle

David Hurdle

David Hurdle

David Hurdle

David Hurdle

**Well-signed cycle routes in Dumfries and the surrounding countryside**

Transport policies from local through to central government all encompass supporting more 'active travel' – cycling and walking. Dumfries and Galloway's Active Travel Strategy states that *"Our vision is to see active travel being the normal choice for short, everyday journeys across all our communities"*; and Scotland's National Transport Strategy published in 2020 states that *"A collaborative approach will be encouraged to ensure all relevant partners work together to make walking and cycling the most popular and preferred mode of travel in Scotland for short journeys"*; and *"We will design our transport system so that walking, cycling and public and shared transport take precedence ahead of private car use."* So, very clear and positive messages for cycling.

Scotland now has an Ambassador for Active Travel, independent of Government, who focuses on championing diverse and inclusive participation in active travel and active travel decision-making. The county of Dumfries and Galloway now has over 724km (450 miles) of signposted cycle routes as well as many off-road cycle trails and world class mountain bike trail centres. The council publishes useful maps.[7]

---

[7] https://www.dumgal.gov.uk/media/17736/Green-Travel-Map-Side-

David Hurdle

**Cycle racks are an important 'welcome' in Scotland's 'National Book Town'**

## And finally…

From all accounts Kirkpatrick was a remarkable yet unassuming and unambitious man, kind-hearted, sympathetic, modest, stern, determined, curious, mild-tempered, a pillar of the local community; content to ride his machine locally and let it be copied by other local mechanics. James Johnston describes

---

1/pdf/Sustainable_Travel_Map.pdf?m=63601594143587
0000

him as *"….of a kindly nature – one of the hail-fellow-well-met sort – a lively companion, and man devoid of any pride. He stood over six feet, a fine specimen of an athlete. And was admittedly a powerful and fearless rider, in fact, one of our earliest trick riders".* His younger sister, Isabella, interviewed in 1892 remembers Kirkpatrick riding through Thornhill on a machine and described him as *"a man of indomitable pluck; once he set himself to any complicated piece of work he persevered until he had successfully mastered it."*

He loved being a blacksmith and working with horses. No tramp or pedlar was ever turned away from his smithy without being given something to eat and drink. He was deeply religious, yet humorous with a boyish sense of fun

Drumlanrig Castle played an important part in Kirkpatrick's life and this link has continued. As well as being a lovely place to cycle to, it has Rik's Shed www.riksbikeshed.co.uk where you can hire bicycles; and electric bikes can be hired in Penpont from the KPT (Keir, Penpont and Tynron) Development Trust info.kptdt@gmail.com.

David Hurdle

**Bikes can be hired at Drumlanrig Castle**

David Hurdle

**And how many places offer a bike wash?!**

The castle has twice been the venue for stage finishes of the national cycle race, the Tour of Britain, loosely modelled on the Tour de France.

There are over 1 billion bicycles in the world today. Kirkpatrick certainly did build better than he knew.

Courtesy Oliver Dixon, www.geograph.org.uk

**Members of a rally on 24th May 2009 halting beside Courthill Smithy to pay their respects en route from a cyclists' breakfast in the village hall to Drumlanrig Castle.**

*"He appeared to drive it with a pair of stirrups or pedals hanging from the fore part of the frame, which were connected by an iron rod to the cranks or axle of hind wheel ....you will have no difficulty in getting information from plenty of the old people in the neighbourhood of Thornhill...."*

**Thomas Haining, farmer in Laight Tynron, letter to The Scottish Cyclist, 17th February 1892**

# BIBLIOGRAPHY

Barr Ian, 2021, The historical tale of Jamesie Burns & the bicycle thieves, Hoggett Creative.

Carroll David, 2000, Old Dumfries, Stenlake Publishing.

Carroll David, 2008, Old Thornhill, Durisdeer, Enterkinfoot, Carronbridge, Keir Mill, Penpont, Tynron, Stenlake Publishing.

Carroll David, 2014, The Dumfries Book of Days, The History Press.

Caunter C F, 1955, The History and Development of Cycles, Part 1 Historical Survey, Her Majesty's Stationery Office.

Colson Ben, 2021, A Journey's End, Ben Colson.

Dinwiddie Robert, 1935, Dinwiddie's Guide to Dumfries.

Dumfries and Galloway Council, 1997, Dumfries Through the Lens, Glimpses of old Thornhill and District.

Irving Gordon, 1986, The Devil on Wheels, Alloway Publishing Ltd.

Johnston James, 1899, The First Bicycle, The Gallovidian, Winter 1899.

Jones Ian, 2012, The Safety Bicycle, Shire Publications.

Kidd Dorothy I, 1992, To See Oursels, Rural Scotland in Old Photographs, HarperCollins Publishers.

Mackinnon Murray and Oram Richard, 2003, The Scots A Photohistory, Thames & Hudson.

McCulloch Andrew, 2018, Dumfriesshire A Frontier Region, Origin.

McGurn J, 1999, On your Bicycle, Open Road.

Mitton G E (Ed.), 1922, Black's Guide to Scotland West and South-West, A & C Black Ltd.

Murray Andy, 1989, Discovering Dumfriesshire, John Donald Publishers Ltd.

Ritchie Andrew, 2009, The Origins of the Bicycle: Kirkpatrick Macmillan, Gavin Dalzell, Alexandre Lefebvre, The John Pinkerton Memorial Publishing Fund.

Tabraham Chris, 2010, The History of Scotland, Colin Baxter Photography Ltd.

The Scottish Motor Traction Co. Ltd, undated, Dumfries and The Land of Burns.

Thornhill Village Committee, undated, A Guide to Thornhill Dumfriesshire.

Waugh Joseph Laing, 1923, Thornhill and its Worthies, Robert Dinwiddie.

# ACKNOWLEDGEMENTS

Dumfries Ewart Library, Dumfries and Galloway Council, especially Alison Burgess, Team Leader, Local Studies and Archives Development Communities, for her assistance with old photographs.

Dumfries Museum and Camera Obscura.

Sophia Harkness, Joseph Thomson Group, Penpont; and Alison Foggie and Marlene Marshall of Keir, for their reading of a draft, valuable comments and a film, see below.

**From a short film '150 years since the pedal bicycle was invented by Kirkpatrick Macmillan at Courthill Smithy', at Penpont School in 1990; and showing a replica being explained.**

# ABOUT THE AUTHOR

David Hurdle DipTP, MA, MRTPI (Rtd), FCILT

 David lives in Sheringham, Norfolk but was born in Dumfries. For his first three months he lived in Thornhill's Buccleuch and Queensberry Hotel, which his grandparents and mother ran. Then he moved to London. He has fond memories of many childhood holidays in Thornhill, learning to cycle on his grandmother's lawn and exploring the area with his dad on hired bikes. They would often cycle past Kirkpatrick's smithy at Keir Mill. Decades later David discovered when tracing his family tree that Kirkpatrick was his uncle's great grandfather's brother-in-law.[8]

---

[8] David's maternal Uncle Bobbie was a son of James Marchbank; *his* father was Robert and *his* father was George. It was George, Bobbie's great grandfather, who married Isabella MacMillan. Isabella was a sister of Kirkpatrick.

David writes a regular public transport column in a monthly magazine in his home town of Sheringham, Norfolk; has written 'Little Bus Stories' for 5 – 7 year olds; and has co-edited 'Road Passenger Transport Management, Planning and Coordinating Passenger Transport Operations' which is all about the bus industry and how local authorities can assist bus operation.

He enjoys cycling still at 76, visits the Thornhill area regularly and hires a bike from Rik's Bike Shed at Drumlanrig Castle. He would recommend Dumfriesshire as a delightful, very cycle-friendly part of Scotland. He hopes readers find this account of Kirkpatrick and his way of life interesting and useful.

Harry Hurdle

**David learning to ride on his grandmother's lawn in 1953**

Printed in Great Britain
by Amazon

39570061R00046